KNOW THE GOD
THROUGH THE LENS OF SCIENCE

AF490628

SURESH KUMAR PAREEK

ISBN 979-8-89475-308-9

Most of us follow some religion or another. Every religion has its own beliefs & the most important belief of all religions is believing in one or multiple deities. Also, there are Atheists who do not believe in God. This book will define the God. I am sure that after reading this book one, whether he is believer or non-believer, will have a clarity in his thought about the God.

Today's India has believers of all the religious faiths. Before we discuss about the God, let's have a brief glimpse of the historical & geographic background of the greater India, which existed before 650 AD. This will provide proper context & will help in easy understanding of the main Concept.

Contents

Ancient History of Greater India

Mishr is the name of Egypt in Egyptian local Masri language. This is also its Indian name & there are many people in India with Mishra as their surname. Surname in Sanskrit is known as 'Jati' & Jati means origin or root.

El- badari is an ancient archaeological site in upper Egypt. This site is dated 4400 BC. The site is named after a nearby town by the same name. There is another archaeological site named El- amra of Amratian culture, 120 KM south of El- badari & is dated 4400 to 3500 BC. The names of both the places- Badari & Amra are Indian. Badrinath & Amarnath are holy places in India. Badrinath and Amra Ram are the names of many Indians.

Ramesside period was the period of 1292 BC to 1077 BC when 11 pharaohs or kings by the names Ramesses 1 to Ramesses 11 ruled Egypt, where Rama is the name of an Indian deity.

Luxor is a governate in Egypt, where Luxor temple is situated. Lakshmana is the brother of Lord Rama. The words Lakshmana & Luxor have the same origin. The ancient city of Waset is located in Luxor, Where Vasishta is the name of the Guru of Lord Rama. Vashishtiputra Satakarni was ruler of Deccan India during the 2nd century CE, whose name is derived from Waset.

Abu Simbel is a massive rock-cut temple created by cutting solid rock cliffs during the reign of Ramesses II. It is located in the Aswan governate of southern Egypt. This indicates the high level of tools & electronic technology available during the period of around 1250 BC. The temple entrance has 4 no. of 66 ft high stone statues.

Similar technology is used in the Kailasa Temple of Ellora in India. Abu is stated as the origin place of the 4 Kshatriya clans of India. The word Aswan is derived from the Sanskrit word Ashwa, meaning a Horse. Twin Ashwani kumaras are revered in Indian texts.

Southern Egypt & northern Sudan were ruled by the kingdom of Kush, established in 1070 BC. Kush is the name son of Lord Rama. Also, there are people in India by surname Kushwaha & Kachhwaha, who claims to be descendants of Lord Rama.

Indian surname Bayya (Biya) originated from the country name of Libya. Surname Nayak (Naik) originated from the Cyrenaica province of Libya.

Babar is a municipality in Khenchela province of Algeria. Indian surname Babar is derived from this.

There was a kingdom of Berber people in present-day Algeria & from this word Barbaric is derived. Barbaric is Indian deity popularly known by name Khathu Shyamji.

East from Egypt, in present-day Syria, there is an abandoned port city named Amrit. Amrit is a Sanskrit word meaning Nectar.

Sumer was one of the oldest civilisations. Its archaeological sites, like Ur & Kish, are situated in present-day southern Iraq. In Hindu mythology, Sumeru is the center of the world. Sumerians kept everything recorded in clay tablets.

Enmebaragesi & lugal- zage- si ruled Sumeria around 2900 BC & 2400 BC respectively. Inspired by the name of Keshi, Lord Krishna got the name Keshava. Kassites ruled Sumeria from 1500 to 1150 BC. Kassites had rulers by the name Agum, Burnaburiash & Maruttash, which resemble Indian names Agam, Purna Puri-isha & Maruta. Kassites rulers considered them as descendants of Shuqamuna. Similarly, there is a surname in India called Keshote. Keshotes consider themselves descendants of Shuka Muni. During 2300 BC, a great King, Sargon Akkad, ruled Sumeria, followed by his son Rimush. The names are similar to Indian names Sirjan Heggade & Ramesh. Lord Krishna's name, Kishan, is inspired by the name of Sumerian, city of Kish. A unicorn seal of Indus Valley civilisation is excavated from Kish; this reflects the relation between Sumer and Indus Valley civilisation. Indian surname Inania is derived from the name of the Sumerian deity Inanna. Seleucia is the name of an ancient city in the Baghdad governorate of Iraq. Solanki & Chalukya are Indian surnames & they are derived from Seleucia. Similarly, Baghela & Bagundya surnames are derived from Baghdad. Wasit is the name of a governorate in Iraq. This name is a distorted form of Vasishta, an ancient Indian sage.

Indian surname Sakaranya is derived from the Sakarya River of present-day Turkey. Indian surnames Kapadia and Kapdoda are derived from the Cappadocia region of Turkey. Bhrigu was an ancient sage. The name of the ancient kingdom of Phrygia is derived from Bhrigu. Phrygia is situated in today's central Turkey. Indian surname Bhargava is derived from Phrygia.

Here, kindly note that the letter 'Bha' is pronounced as 'Pha' in Greek records. For example, the name of King Subhagasena, who ruled Kabul during the 3rd century BC, is pronounced Sophagasenus.

The Kingdom of Pontus was ruled by the Mithridatic dynasty in northern Turkey from 281 BC to 63 BC. Six kings of this dynasty were named as Mithridates or Mithra dutt. The word Pontus is spelled in the epic Mahabharata as King Pandu of Hastinapur. The word Hastinapur is derived from the ancient Hittite (Hatti) empire, which ruled most of modern Turkey from 1600 BC to 1200 BC. Hathi means Elephant & Hastinapur means place of elephants. Surnames like Pandya, Panda, Pandey & Pant are derived from Pontus. The popular Pandian dynasty ruled southern Tamil Nadu for a long period. Earlier name of Tamil Nadu was Madras. Its earlier capital was Madurai. Both words- Madras & Madurai are derived from the name of Pandu's wife Madri.

In the east, in Iran, the great Parthian or Arsacid empire existed from 247 BC to 224 AD. Most of the rulers of this dynasty were named as Mithridates (Mitra Dutt) or Phrates (Bharath). In brackets, Hindu names of the kings are written, which are very much Indian. In the year 57 BC, there was a change of ruler of this dynasty, where Orodes II (Viru) took charge. This matches with the beginning of the Vikram Samvat calendar, which started in 57 BC. Vikram Samvat is the most popular calendar in India. The word Parthian is derived from the word Parth or Arjuna of Mahabharata. From the word Arsacid is derived the Kannada word Arasa, which means King. Arasa is the title used by the kings of Mysore. A branch of Parthians also ruled over the land, presently known as Armenia. Parthians ruled the area previously ruled by Cyrus (Kuru) the Great, so the Arjuna is called Kuruvanshi. The Parthian shot is the idiom for the best arrow shot. Arjuna is said to be the best archer in the world, as per the epic Mahabharata.

Parthian rule was followed by Sasanians, who ruled Iran from 224 AD to 651 AD. Six of these rulers were named Bahram, where Ram was the last name of the kings & 2 were named Narsieh (Narsi), which are Hindu names. There is also a town named Ramsar in northern Iran. Darius the Great is remembered in Indian texts as Durvasa rishi. Bazarangids ruled Fars

& Kerman of Iran, whereas Bajarang Bali is the name of the popular Hindu deity Hanuman.

Mohen jo Daro is an archaeological site in Sindh, Pakistan. The word means Mohan's mound, in Sindhi language. Mohan is the name of the Hindu deity Krishna. Even today, the people living around that area are called Mohana.

From the above examples, it is clear that prior to 650AD, the Hindu religion was vastly spread not only in India but in many other countries like Algeria, Libya, Sudan, Egypt, Syria, Turkey, Iraq, Iran, Armenia, Afghanistan, and Pakistan. These countries combined may be called Bharath Varsha.

It was the hard-line & brutal religious expansion of Islam through various Caliphates that forced the Hindu Population, particularly the Rulers, Aristocrats, Priests & their families, to leave their birthplace. Those who could not flee were forcibly converted to Islam. There was a mass migration of those who adhered to their religious faith. Most of them migrated to today's India or Bharath Khanda. A few centuries later, India itself was conquered by Islamic forces.

Once the greater India (Bharath varsha), shrunk to its current size in 1947 CE, with Pakistan & Bangladesh being latest pieces separated from it.

Now, let's come to the main topic.

We can try to understand God in 3 parts: as

1. Physical Entity

2. Time (Kaal)

3. Universal Consciousness

God As A Physical Entity

It is said that God is Omni present, which means he is everywhere. He is there in everything. Prince Prahalad proved this to his father, King Hiranyakashipu.

In Hinduism, Tridev- Brahma, Vishnu & Shiva are considered supreme of all the Gods. Similarly, Christians have a parallel form of Tridev as Trinity, where one is father, the other is son & the another is the Holy Soul. All 3 are Gods, but they are different from each other.

When we look around us, we find living things & Non-living things everywhere. On further analysis, we find that all the things around us are made of matter. Matter is made of chemical compounds & Molecules. Further, these are made of atoms. The hundred-and-odd types of atoms are the building blocks of everything around us. But all the atoms are made of just 3 Particles, namely proton, electron & neutron. For example, a Helium atom is made of 2 protons, 2 electrons & 2 neutrons & Gold atom is made of

79 protons, 79 electrons & 118 neutrons. In general, atoms are unbreakable. But for the sake of understanding, if we break all the types of atoms into basic particles, we find only 3 things- protons, electrons & neutrons. All the protons are just protons; there is no difference in whether they are extracted from Helium, Gold, or some other atom. Similarly, all the electrons are the same. The same holds good for neutrons. Now we can conclude that everything around us is made of just 03 things- proton, electron, & neutron.

The fact is that Brahma of the Tridev, father of Trinity & proton of science book are one & same. Similarly, Vishnu of Tridev, the Holy Soul of the Trinity & electron of science book is one & same. And Shiva of Tridev, son of Trinity & neutron of science book is one & same.

However, a question arises: Is there anything that proves the above statements?

The answer is Yes.

Let's first discuss about Lord Shiva;

Neutron is without positive or negative charge. It is made of one up- Quark (+2/3 charge) & 2 down- quarks (a Total of both have -2/3 charge); the total charge of the neutron is 0. So is Shiva, who is always involved in austerities and is called Ardhanarishwara, meaning half man & half woman (because the total charge is zero).

The 1ˢᵗ stanza of Shiva Bilvastakam, a poem by Adi Shankaracharya & dedicated to Shiva, reads:

Tridalam trigunakaram trinetram cha triyayudham
Trijanmapapasamharam bilvapatram shivarpanam

It means 3 leaves of Aegle marmelos tree, triangle-shaped, three-eyed, and with three weapons, when offered to Shiva, relinquishes from sins of 3 births.

Shiva has got 3 Eyes.

  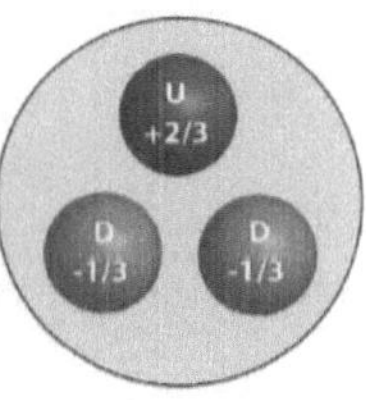

Bilva patra & 3 eyes of Shiva explain the structure of neutron, which is made of 3 quarks (one Up- Quark & 2 down- quarks).

A neutron is a half-spin particle. Shiva holds Damaru, or Drum, which also spins half.

The Standard Model of particle physics (which explains that a neutron is made of 3 quarks) was introduced in the year 1975. But Lord Shiva is revered in this form since time immemorial.

Lord Vishnu lives in Vaikuntha loka, & The word Vaikuntha means adobe, which is cornerless. He is depicted as resting on a serpent's coil, which is also circular. He holds discuss as a Weapon, which always orbits around a point. His vehicle is Garuda (a Vulture), who flies orbiting around Carcasses in a circular path. Electrons always orbit around the nucleus in a circular or cornerless path. Viakuntha loka has 7 boundaries; electrons have 7 orbits. Vishnu Loka is visited by 4 rishi kumaras: Sanaka, Sanandana, Sanatana, and Sanatkumara. Electrons are also bound to be in 4 orbitals or blocks- s, p, d & f. Vishnu Loka has 2 guards- Jaya & Vijaya. Electrons also always exist in a pair of 2.

In the Hindu marriage ritual (a ritual of forming a pair of 2 individuals), Lord Vishnu is praised by the mantra, with the seven-time circling of the wedding couple around the holy fire-

Mangalam Bhagwan Vishnuh, Mangalam Garudadhwajah
Mangalam Pundari Kakshah, Mangalaya Tano Harih

This represents 7 orbits of electrons. In western Rajasthan, the couple circle around the holy fire only 4 times. This represents 4 orbitals of the Electron. Lord Visnu is known as 'Palan Kartha' or the sustainer of the world. This is true, as the electrons are behind every chemical reaction, resulting in the formation of all chemical molecules or compounds, whether organic or inorganic. The electrons are the cause of all-electric & electronic activities.

This establishes that Lord Vishnu is present in every atom as an electron & he is the sustainer of the world.

For example, when Table Salt is added with concentrated Sulphuric Acid, it produces sodium Bisulphate and Hydrochloric acid, but when the same Table Salt is added with diluted Sulphuric Acid, it produces sodium Sulfate and Hydrochloric acid.

It means that electrons, which are behind every chemical reaction, act differently in different conditions & they have decision-making ability or consciousness.

There is a famous temple in Kerala's capital, Thiruvananthapuram, known as Padmanabha Swamy temple. The word Thiruvananthapuram means place of 3, who are infinite. The word Padmanabha swamy means the Lord who has lotus in his Navel or Nucleus. This temple is dedicated to Lord Vishnu. A large statue of Vishnu sleeping on coils of 7 hooded serpents is depicted as having a lotus arising from his navel & Lord Brahma sitting on the lotus. A similar statue of Lord Vishnu is there in Ranganatha Swamy temple, Tirupati. The coils of the hooded serpent represent

7 orbits of electrons in an atom. Words- Allah & electron have same root of origin, that is ilahi.

This depicts that Lord Brahma lives in the Navel or Nucleus of Lord Vishnu. The same is the case with proton. Protons are found in the nucleus of an atom & the nucleus is surrounded by electrons. Lord Brahma has got 4 faces. Similarly, a proton has 3 quarks & a positive charge, which represents 4 faces.

This clarifies that every matter available in the universe is made of 3 basic particles & these are part of Lord Brahma, Lord Vishnu & Lord Shiva.

Now, the next question arises about the origin of the 3 Immortals & the answer lies in the Theory of the Birth of Matter, which goes as follows-

Our Solar system is an open system. This means the Sun interacts with outer space. The Sun is surrounded by a river of Interstellar medium, which flows from the direction of star Antares. Inspired by the name of the star Antares, the outer space is called Antariksha.

In aarti of Jagadish ji, it is stated for God-

Tum Pooran paramatma, Tum antar yami

This means the Lord is complete in himself & he is moving from the direction of Antares.

This Interstellar plasma enters the Solar system through solar bow shock and flows toward the Sun over solar poles. With the help of the fast rotation of the Solar surface, this plasma flows throughout the Solar system like a disk. This flow is known as Solar wind. This Solar wind consists of the interplanetary magnetic field, which interacts with & is received by planets through their bow shocks & over their poles. Interplanetary magnetic field is free-flowing energy. I will call this energy Amba. Magnet is called Chumbak in Sanskrit. The word Chumbak is made of the basic word Amba with the prefix Chu & suffix Ak. It is similar to another word- Krishak, in its tone. The basic word Krishi means agriculture & suffix Ak makes it agriculturist. Amba means the energy in the form of a magnetic field.

The Earth's Magnetosphere is Shaped like a Shiva lingam. This Magnetosphere interacts with an interplanetary magnetic field. This looks like 'Abhisheka' of Shivalinga with Amba.

(*Image courtesy: NASA*)

That is why people do abhisheka of Shivalinga with water. Where Shiva lingam represents the Magnetosphere, & The water represents the Amba or interplanetary magnetic field. Note here that water is also called Ambu.

Lord Shiva holds a new moon over his forehead. Since Earth's Magnetosphere is always directed toward the Sun, the new moon looks as if it is held over the Shiva lingam.

The Magnetosphere of Other Planets & Sun are also shaped like Shiva lingam.

From the poles, this Amba enters into the core of the planets. The flow of Amba from the poles to the core is along magnetic lines. In the core of the planets, huge quantities of negatively & Positively charged Amba join together to form known particles like quarks, electrons, protons, neutrons, etc. Later, these newly formed particles join in various combinations to form various atoms & molecules. This process of the birth of matter is similar to the process of formation of a living being from the yolk inside an Egg.

A Rajasthani devotional song known as 'Chosath Jogani' expresses the birth of Brahma (proton), Vishnu (Electron), Shiva (neutron), Shakti (Energy) & Six headed Kartikeya (Six types of quarks) from Jagadamba or Amba.

There is a dynasty in Puranas called Bharathas. The marriage of Bharata prince Vichitraviya with 2 daughters of Kashi Naresh- Ambika & Ambalika refers to two types of solar winds- fast solar wind & slow solar wind, and the Amba refers to interplanetary magnetic field.

The word Bharatha originates from Bharat. And Bharat means something which fills this world. There is a mention of jad-bharat in Srimadbhagat Gita & the word jad means root or base of everything.

This clarifies the origin of the 3 immortals is from Amba.

Dattatreya

Another question arises- if the trio are living ones, do they consume anything? The answer lies in the Theory of neutrino absorption by atomic particles, which states-

1. Atoms absorb solar neutrinos.

2. They do so to set off the energy lost by 3 atomic particles- electrons, protons & neutrons, due to their spin.

The Great Pyramid of Giza is the tomb of pharaoh Khufu, built around 2600 BC, and is, in fact, dedicated to the solar God Ra. Ra arose as the main deity during that period. 'Ra' means solar ray. The pyramid is designed in such a way that when we see a cross-section of it, we find that its upper shaft or opening shows the refraction of light in the same way as the light is refracted by a prism. A pyramid made of glass refracts light in the same way a prism does.

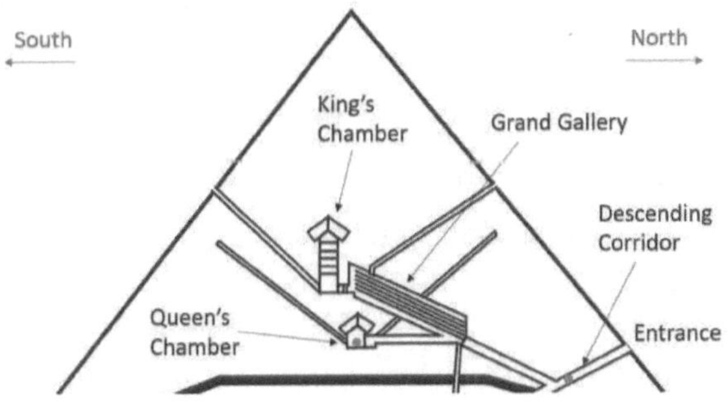

(Image courtesy: Quora.com)

The upper shaft is connected to the King's chamber. There is a lower shaft in the pyramid, whose both ends are closed. This lower shaft is connected to the Queen's chamber, which in turn is connected to the Earth. This design of the pyramid's upper shaft reveals that photons of sunlight are refracted to the atmosphere & do not enter the Earth; the lower shaft, closed at both ends, reveals that solar neutrinos don't refract but penetrate the surface & enter the Earth. In the epic

Uttara Ramayana, at the end, Sita, the Queen, enters the Earth, but Ram, the King, is unable to do so. The Egyptian King named Ramesses- 1 represents God Ra or sun ray & his Queen Sitre represents neutrino.

It means Ramesses- 1 or Ram represents photon. In Sri Ram stuti, a devotional poem, Rama is called as-.

Navami, Janak suta Varam

Where Navami means Nine. Here, He is denoted by 9 frequencies of light, the 7 colors of rainbow, Infra-red & Ultraviolet. Similarly, the Sun God in Hindu temples is depicted as riding on 7 Horses of 7 rainbow colors. Below verse from 'Bal kand' of Ram Charit Manas written by Tulasi Das clarifies that Lord Ram stands for Sun light-

"Sab kar param prakashak joi, Ram anaadi avadhpati soi"

Meaning that the one who provides light to all is Ram, the Lord of Ayodhya. Note down here that the city name Ayodhya is derived from an ancient Egyptian city called Abydos, meaning invincible in Sanskrit.

Below is one more example from Ram Charit Manas, where Ram is called as light-

"Jagat prakashya prakashak ramu, mayadheesh gyan gun dhamu"

'Janak suta varam' in the previous verse means husband of Sita. Sitre or Sita, represents neutrino. The word Sita means cooler one. For neutrinos, it is true, as they do not increase the temperature of a surface with which they come in contact. In contrast, photons increase the surface temperature.

In the epic Ram Charit Manas, there is a verse-

"Anasuya ke pad gai Sita, mili bahori Susheel vineeta"

Here, Sita is said to be following Anasuya's steps. Meaning that Sita & Anasuya are same.

In Puranic stories, Anasuya is stated as one who fed the three- Brahma, Vishnu, & Shiva. It means neutrinos feed protons, electrons & neutrons.

The word Anasuya means the invisible one, which is true for neutrinos. There is an Indian deity named Dattatreya, with 3 heads & single body; he represents Brahma, Vishnu & Shiva in a single body, that is, proton, electron & neutron in a single body of the atom. Lord Dattatreya is son of sage Atri & Anasuya. The word Datta means adopted son, & treya means three. This means that the three-headed God was not born to Anasuya but was adopted by her. This is true as 3 atomic particles are born from Amba. Since Anasuya feeds them, so she is their adoptive mother. There were many kings named Tiridates in ancient Armenia

& Parthia, who got this name inspired by the name of Dattatreya.

In the poem Vishnu Sahasranama written by Rishi Vyasa, there is a stanza-

"Sahasranam tad tulyam Ram nam vara nane, Ram nam vara nana om iti"

This means that after a thousand names, Nana, the consort of Rama, is weighed.

In the epic Ramcharitmanas, Ram has only one wife, that is Sita. This means like Anasuya, Nana is another name for Sita or neutrino. The word Nana means tiny or very small, which is true for neutrinos. A tiny Particle in English is also called a Nano-particle.

But who is Nana? How do you weigh Nana?

The answer comes from ancient Sumeria. Inanna was an ancient deity there. There is a poem, 'Inanna's Journey to the underworld,' wherein the goddess is taken captive in the underworld. Later, she was released with a condition that her husband dumuzid or damu and damu's sister would become captive in the underworld, alternately. This means two-thirds are kept captive.

Similarly, in Sudama Charitra, Krishna consumes two-thirds of the rice offered by Sudama when he meets Vasudeva Krishna in Dwarka. Here, su-dama represents the damu of the Sumerian story, and Vasudeva represents the Earth. By the way, Susheela is Sudama's wife. The name Susheel is mentioned in the above verse of the epic Ramcharitmanas.

Here, a question arises about whether Krishna really represents Earth.

Krishna is the eighth & last son of his mother, Devaki. This means Devaki has Eight sons. So, there are 8 planets in our Solar system. In Puranas, there are 8 Gods, known as Vasus or Asta-Vasus. Krishna is also called Vasudeva. The word Vasudeva means Provider of shelter. The word Krishna is derived from 'Krishi' or agriculture, where Krishak means agriculturist & Krishna means the Earth on which agriculture is practiced. There is another name for Lord Krishna-Bankebihari, which means 'One who moves in a tilted manner.' This holds good for Earth, as it moves around the sun at a tilt on its axis by 23.5 degrees. Krishna is adorned with a type of Peacock feather known as Chandava. Earth has one natural satellite, Chandrama, or the moon.

By a combination of all the above stories from Puranas, we can summarize that Sita, Nana, Anasuya & Sudama are the names for the invisible solar neutrino & 2 third of the neutrinos coming to Earth are absorbed by electrons, neutrons & protons of atoms present in the Earth. Since the atomic particles lose energy due to their spin, they absorb neutrinos passing by them to recover the lost energy.

Now it is clear the trio do spin, or the Tridev are indulged in cosmic dance & consume neutrinos. It means that they have a life but it is little different from ours.

In Hindu mythology, Lord Brahma is known as param pita or the father of all, and the universe as a whole is known as Brahmanda. In western mythology, the Trinity has 3 persons: Father, son & Holy Soul. Is there any mention in the scriptures which clarifies this?

There is a story in Puranas about a Yagna or Sacrifice by Prajapati Daksha, a son of Brahma. In this Yagna, King Daksha invites Brahma & Vishnu but intentionally does not invite Shiva. Hydrogen is the most abundant element in the universe, accounting for 75% of normal matter. Hydrogen is made of only 2 particles: Proton & Electron. There is no neutron in Hydrogen. And if we talk about the mass of the proton & Electron, we find that most of the mass is of the proton & that of the Electron is nominal. This is why the universe is called Brahmanda; it is made of Brahma tattva or protons.

Sun is made mostly of hydrogen. There, Hydrogen elements join to produce Helium & energy. In this nuclear reaction, one- up quark of proton converts into one down and & hence, one proton is converted into a neutron. Thereby making Helium, which has 2 protons, 2 electrons & 2 neutrons. This is why proton, which produces, is called father, neutron, which is produced, is called son & electron, which is indifferent, is called the Holy Soul. The Energy or Shakti produced here is called the daughter of King Daksha or granddaughter of Lord Brahma. This Energy is spread toward all directions, which are known by 27 nakshatras & each of the Nakshatra has 4 padas, making a total of 108 divisions or a full 360-degree circle. To remember this phenomenon, there are 108 Shakti peethas.

Then, a question arises: Is Earth a living thing?

Earth's continents move or drift relative to each other over geologic time. This is studied as the science of plate tectonics. This phenomenon is confirmed by earthquakes occurring at the edges of various lithospheric plates of Earth. The Movements of continents are like stages of development of an Egg. This is why Krishna is called the eighth Garbha of Devaki, where Garbha means embryo.

Omkar

The word Omkar is made by a combination of 2 words, Aum & Kar. Where Aum is the name & Kar means line. From this is derived The Greeting 'Namaskar'. In science, Omkar is represented by the surface current of thermohaline circulation. This is a unique Stream of Oceanic water flowing in the shape of Aum. It covers all the oceans from the North Pole to the South Pole. The property of water flowing in thermohaline circulation is different from the surrounding oceanic water, as it transports heat, salt & ions between mid-oceans & poles.

In the epic Mahabharata, this stream is named as Draupadi. The word Draupadi is made from 2 words, Drav & pathi, meaning Lord of liquid (Water).

In the epic Ramayana, this stream is discussed when Sugriva want to test the might of Lord Rama before killing Bali. He asks Rama to pierce the seven trees in a single arrow shot & Rama does it successfully. The Seven trees are the 7 oceans of Earth & Rama's arrow is the Omkar Stream.

Again, just before making a bridge to reach Lanka, Rama asks the ocean to give him the way to march to Lanka. Ocean denies Rama & puts forth his inability to do so as he (ocean) is a jad or dead thing. Then Rama fires an arrow shot in the northern direction. This northern direction is the North Pole & the arrow shot of Rama is the Omkar stream.

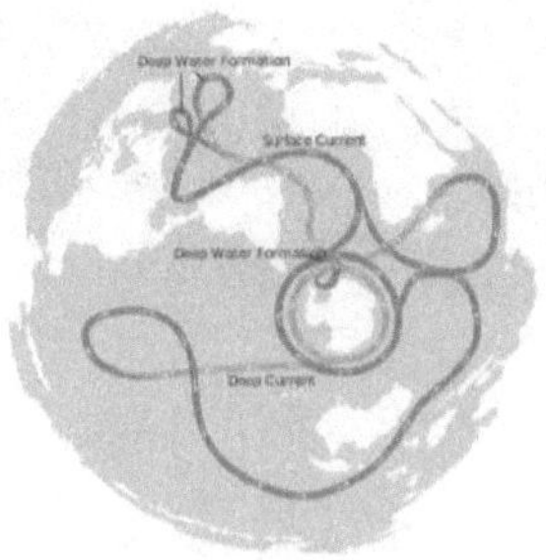

(Image courtesy: Wikipedia)

The thermohaline circulation was found by scientists in the year 1960, but Omkar has been revered by Hindus since time immemorial. Abrahamic faiths also have words like Amen and Ameen.

Earth's atmospheric temperature varies at different altitudes of the atmosphere. Tropopause at an altitude of 10 KM has a temperature of -55 degrees; Stratopause at an altitude of 50 KM has a temperature of 0 degrees; Mesopause at an altitude of 85 KM has a temperature of -90 degrees, followed by Thermosphere at an altitude of 120 KM has a temperature of +80 degree. This kind of variation of minus, plus, minus & plus temperature patterns at various altitudes is possible for living things.

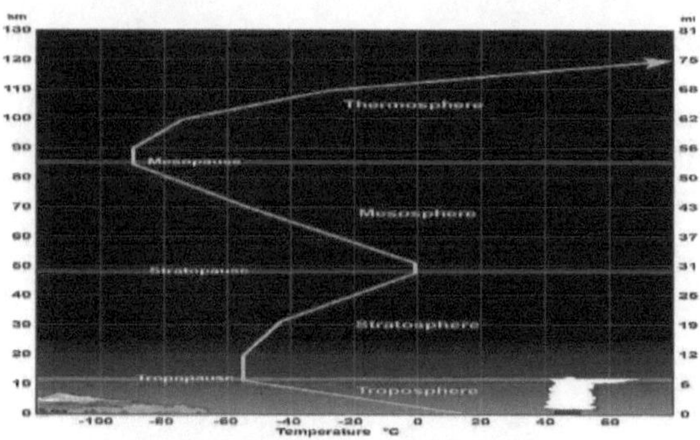

(Image courtesy: NOAA.gov, USA)

Earth orbits around the sun in a circular manner. But the bow shock of Earth is always directed toward Sun. It means that bow shock turns 90 degrees every 3 months & 360 degrees every year. The magnetic lines of bow shock interact with the interplanetary magnetic field.

This is possible only if Earth is a living thing.

Many sun-grazing comets, particularly Kreutz group comets, pass extremely close to the Sun at their perihelion; sometimes, they enter the solar surface. Although small sungrazers can completely evaporate during close approach to the Sun, larger sungrazers can survive many perihelion passages. The strong evaporation and tidal forces they experience often lead to the fragmentation & formation (birth) of new comets.

Like comets, other planets also have some kind of tail. For example, our moon has a sodium ion tail, which covers the Earth's surface every no-moon day, especially during solar eclipses. Mercury also has a sodium ion tail. Venus has a gas tail, which extends up to the surface of the Earth when Venus is synodic with the Earth. Our Earth also has a magnetic tail. That is why in the epic Ramayana, Rama is shown to have a full army of Monkeys.

Lord Hanuman is praised in the poem Hanuman Bahuk as

Atulit Baldhamam Hem Shelabhdeham

Meaning the very powerful body of Ice & Stones.

In his arti, Hanuman is praised as

Vajr Deh Danav Dalan, Jai Jai Jai kapi Sur

This means with the body of Vajra or Sand (Bajari) slayer of Danavas, hail the one with tail (Monkey).

The above stanzas clarify that Lord Hanuman is a Sungrazer Comet because only Sun Grazer comet fulfills the above statements. There is a mention of the birth of Makaradhwaja from Lord Hanuman, a Brahmachari (Unmarried). This is similar to the birth of a new comet.

Many times, sungrazer comets approach very close to the solar surface but do not orbit the sun or go to the other side of the Sun. This means they do not obey the basic principle of orbit around a star. This is only possible when these comets intentionally manage their path of movement during their orbit and change the path using their tail. For example, a Kreutz group comet passed by the solar surface without orbiting the sun on 10th May 2021.

And this is possible only when the comet is a living thing.

God As Time (Kaal)

Earth rotates on its axis for a period of 24 hours. A Constellation in the far north, called Ursa Major, looks like (to the people living in the northern hemisphere) rotating surrounding the Pole star. This rotation of Ursa Major or the Plow or Saptarishis (seven Sages) is drawn in Hindu & Jain rituals as Swastika.

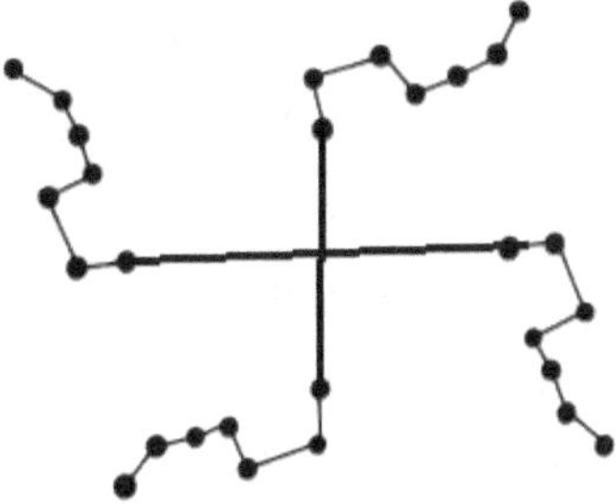

The time of a week is divided into 112 parts, each of an average of one & half hours, named Choghadia. There are 8 Choghadias in a Day & 8 in a Night. This is to remember the average 112-day Solar flare cycle; wherein solar flares increase & decrease during the period of average 112 days.

Basically, these Choghadias are only seven. These 7 repeats in different order in days & nights. The first one of a given day is the same as the last one. So, one Choghadiya is assigned for each Day of the Week.

A Month in Hindu calendar is a lunar synodic month, which is made of 2 fortnights, one of waxing & another of waning moon. After every 33 Months, a month is added & this additional 34th month is called as Purushottam month & during this month special poojas are offered to Gods. This exercise is to match lunar months with the solar months.

In the Hindu calendar, there is only one festival based on solar movement, which is called Makar Sankranti, which falls in mid-January. On this day, the Sun enters Makara rashi or Capricorn zodiac, which means the Sun starts moving Northwards. The important thing to remember about this festival is that married Women in western India distribute 13 gifts to other Women. This gift is called Terunda. The significance of the 13 gifts is that each gift refers to one week. Approximately after the next 13 Weeks, the Hindu New Year is celebrated.

This is the time when solar rays straightly fall on Earth's equator. The New Year starts from the new Moon of Chaitra month. The month of Chaitra is called so because the full moon of this month is in Chitra nakshatra, which is a part of the Kanya Rashi or Virgo constellation. The same rule applies to the other 11 months, which are named after the name of nakshatras. These nakshatras are- Vishakha, Jyeshta, Aashaadha, Shraavana, Bhadrapada, Ashwin, Kritika, Mrigashira, Pushya, Magha & Phalguna. The New Year celebration is for 9 days, so it is called Navaratra, Where Ratra refers to night or 9 nights. The deity of this festival is Durga, which is also called Nava Durga, which denotes a spectrum of sunlight- seven visible colors of the rainbow, one infra-red & one ultraviolet this is how totalling to 9 frequencies of light. On the ninth day, in Abhijit muhurta, Rama Navami is celebrated Since Rama also refers to sun rays. Abhijit muhurta is the time when the Sun is overhead, around 12:30 noon. On the ninth day, 9 virgin Girls are offered Prasadam or Food. Where 9 comes from 9 frequencies of sunlight & virgin Girls refers to the Virgo constellation. Goddess Durga is praised as light in the below stanza, taken from Durga Chalisa-

'Nirankar he jyoti tumhari, tinhu lok faili ujiyari'

This means that your divine light is formless and spreads in 3 Lokas.

Here a doubt arises in mind that why so importance is given to a common natural phenomenon like light, why goddess Durga or Lord Rama are given importance more than all other Gods.

The answer lies in Jware, a plant of Barley seed. The Barley seeds are sown during Navaratri & Barely plants are grown. This reflects the science behind this festival. The growth of plants needs soil, water, air & sunlight. Leaves of plants cook their food, which is glucose, with the help of photons of sunlight by using water & carbon dioxide. Glucose does carry energy inherited from the photons. This energy is the starting point of the food cycle of all the plants & animals of the Earth. This means that without sunlight, there is no food available to plants or animals; hence, there is no life on the Earth.

After 13 plus 13, that is 26 weeks approximately will be celebrated another Navaratri. This time it is Sun coming back from northern hemisphere & it's rays again falling straight over Equator. This time it is Ashwin month. This time also Celebrations are similar to Chaitra Navaratri. Except, instead of Rama Navami, on tenth day Dashahara is celebrated as triumph of Lord Rama. This is the time when the Sun is in the Virgo Zodiac.

After approximately another 13 weeks is another Makara Sankranti. This is how a cycle of 12 months or

52 weeks is completed. There are total of 52 Bhairavas worshipped by Hindus. This matches with 52 weeks of a year. So, there is one Bhairava as the deity of time of one week. One week's time looks like a simple thing, but it is not so. In a week's time, our sun travels 200 KM from north to south or vice versa over the Earth's surface. So, there is a 200 KM shift in temperature, rainfall over the Earth & change in the climate of the Earth.

But, mainly, 2 Bhairavas- Black (Kaala) & White (Gora) are worshipped. The six-month journey of the Sun in the northern Hemisphere is referred to as Gora Bhairav & that in the Southern Hemisphere is Kaala Bhairav.

In singular form, Bhairava is called Kaal Bhairava (Lord of time).

The name of 52 Bhairava is always associated with 64 Yoginis. Like Bhairavas, Yoginis are also deities of time. The word Yogini is made of the basic word yuga. Sixty-four Navaratri refers to 64 Yogas. Since Navaratri is celebrated every 6 months, it means chosath Yoginis combinedly refers to the deities of a period of 32 years. But why 32 years?

The answer is that there are 3 inner planets in our Solar system, other than Earth. They are- Mercury, Venus, Mars & the fourth dwarf planet, ceres, which lies in the Asteroid belt. The average synodic period of these planets with the Earth is synchronized in such a way that- Mercury becomes synodic with the Sun & Earth 101 times, ceres 25 times, Venus 20 times & Mars 15 times during a period of 32 years.

On average, Venus becomes synodic with Earth & Sun 5 times in an eight-year cycle. When this movement of Venus is drawn on paper, it forms the structure of a flower with 5 Petals. This is why flowers are offered to deities during poojas. This also confirms the numbers selected by Lord Buddha for his teachings- Panchasheel for 5 synods & Asthangic marg for the period of 8 Years.

Goddess Gayatri has 5 faces, matching the 5 petals of Venus. Mithridates, or Mitra Datta, King of Parthia, represents Rishi Vishva-Mitra. Scriptures say that Vishva-Mitra is the creator of Gayatri Mantra.

In Jainism, 5 Mahavratas (or 5 great Vows) are defined for Ascetics. Ancient Sumerian deity Ishtar is addressed as a star with 8 angles or an Octa gram, which reflects the eight-year synodic cycle of Venus. In Islam, there is a provision for offering Namaz 5 times a day. This is derived from the 5 synods of Venus. Namaz or prayer is specially offered on Friday. Friday, or Shukravara, is the day of Venus or Shukra Graha. This period of 8 years is also marked by 99 synodic lunar months, which are referred to in scriptures as 99 fire sacrifices by King Prithu. Earth's name, Prithvi, is derived from Prithu. It is important to note here that the Islamic Rosary (Japa Mala) has 99 beads. That is not all; the same duration is marked by 106 perigee to perigee lunar months. Venus is visible in the east during the early morning as the Morning star, when it is at its western greatest elongation. Similarly, it is visible in the west as the evening star during its eastern greatest elongation. Between the 2 greatest elongations are 2 conjunctions of the Venus, one inferior conjunction & another being a superior conjunction. So, in an eight-year cycle, Venus becomes visible 5 times as the morning star & 5 times as the evening star. This phenomenon of Venus is represented by 10 faces of Ravana, also known as Dashanana, a character of Ramayana.

Ravana is said to belong to the Brahmin community. Five appearances of Venus as a morning star are reflected in casts of north Indian Brahmins as Pancha goda Brahmins. The other 5 appearances of Venus as an evening star are reflected in casts of south Indian Brahmins, such as Pancha Dravida Brahmins. When calculated for the main cycle of 32 years, Venus appears & disappears 40 times. This 40 times of appearance & disappearance is the base of the cycle of birth & death in Abrahamic religions. This is why they mourn for the dead persons for 40 days.

Mars becomes synodic with Earth & Sun for 7 times in a period of about 15 years. When this movement of Mars is drawn on paper, it forms the structure of a Kalasha or Pitcher pot with 5 leaves. That is why during all important occasions or Hindu festivals Ghat sthapana or Kalash sthapana is done (A waterfilled Pitcher pot with leaves & coconut kept on that, is installed as a deity). There is a famous temple dedicated to Mars, known as the Mangala Devi temple, in Mangalore.

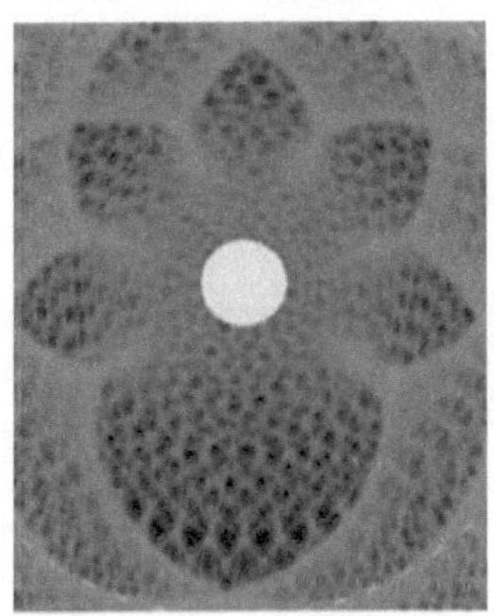 

The above image shows the geometry formed by the movement of Earth & Mars around the Sun. The next image shows Mangal Kalash, which is installed during festivities.

Mercury's 101 synods in a 32-year period appear in the scriptures as a hundred sons & one grandson of Rishi Vasishta. Number 101 appears in Mahabharata as Duryodhana, etc. hundred & Yuyutsu as the 101st son of Dhratarastra. Kindly note that the phonetics of the word Dhratarastra are the same as those of Zarathustra (Zoroaster), founder of the ancient Zoroastrianism religion.

This is in contrast to 5 synods of Venus referring to 5 Pandeva's, the winners of Mahabharata war, sons of King Pandu. Pandu is said to be the founder of Santana Dharma (Hindu religion).

But Mercury offers something better than the synodic cycle. Mercury displays a very interesting transit cycle. Wherein Mercury passes in front of the Solar disk & behind the Sun. Mercury's transit is in a cyclic period of 46 years, wherein there are 12 transits. Six sub-cycles of 46 years each make a main cycle of 2 hundred & 76 years, where the last sub-cycle of 46 years has 13 transits. That means a total of 73 transits in 2 hundred & 76 years. There is a Buddhist scripture in the Pali language known as Patisambhidamagga (meaning path of discrimination). In the first division of this book, known as Mahavagga (Great division), 73 types of Gnana (Knowledge) are described. This number matches with 73 transits of Mercury.

When we analyze the Mercury's transit cycle, we find that there should be total of 103 transits in 276-year period. And we have to remove 5 transits in every sub cycle of 46 years. This removal of 5 transits from the list is remembered as 5 Panchakas.

On the basis of these repetitive transit cycles of Mercury, karmakandas of the afterlife & rebirth are created. Since there are 12 transits in a sub-cycle, there is the ritual of mourning for the dead for 12 days. The sixth sub-cycle has 13 transits, so the 13th day after death is observed as Chhamasi (Six months). The 5 transits, which did not happen, are observed by taking 5 bones of a dead person & immersing them in the river.

In mythological history, there are 3 main instances of the building of a ship. 1st by Manu, whose ship was dragged by Lord Vishnu's incarnation Matsya avatar (in the form of Fish). 2nd one was built by the Sumerian hero Gilgamesh. It is described that he used 3 times 3600 units of Bitumen to build the ship. We just take 36 instead of 3600 units. When 36 is multiplied by 3, we get 108.

Other than this instance, 108 appears when Solar distance from Earth is divided by solar diameter; we get a value of approximate 108. Similarly, When the lunar distance from the Earth is divided by the lunar diameter, we get a value of approximate 108.

But this time, 36 is specifically mentioned. When we divide the value of 10 orbits of ceres by ceres's synodic period, we get 36. And 3 times, in 30 orbits, we get 108 oppositions of ceres. Note that opposition of a planet is when the planet is visible from the Earth in the direction opposite to the Sun. This matches with 108 Nakshatra Padas (there are 27 nakshatras & each one has got 4 padas). This is why there are 108 Beads in Japa Mala (loop of prayer beads). In 100 orbits, we get a value of 360 synods, which refers to 360 degrees. Since this message was spread by Chalukyas, they are called by the name Solanki. Where 'So' stands for 100. Gilgamesh refers to the dwarf planet ceres. There are 2 Temples of Gilgamesh named as Galaganatha temple, both built by Chalukya Kings, One in Haveri & another in Pattadakal., both in Karnataka state. The word Galage in the Kannada language means a unit of time.

Here, it's important to note that the period of 10 orbits of ceres is 46 years, which is equal to Mercury's transit sub-cycle of 46 years.

3rd instance of ship making is by Noah. This ship came down to the Earth's surface after 601 years. Moon moves up by 10 times its diameter & down by 10 times its diameter during its orbit around Earth when compared to Earth's orbital path around the Sun. On average, the mid-point of the eclipse season of the moon is 173.3 days. When there is a full moon on the lunar mid-point, it's a lunar eclipse; if it is no moon day, it's a Solar eclipse. There are 38 such cycles of 173.3 days in 18 years & 11 days. That is why, after 38 cycles, a similar eclipse occurs. But, because of the difference of 10 days & 23 hours, the place of visibility of the Eclipse is changed on Earth's surface. When this

38 cycle's value is multiplied by 33.333, we get a period of 601 years. This time, the eclipse will occur in the same place. And this is the period when Noah's ships come down back to the Earth's surface.

Kindly note that the period of 291 seasons of 173.3 days each is equal to 108 oppositions of ceres, with a difference of one lunation. Where 108 oppositions of ceres stand for 108 beads of Japa Mala & one additional lunation stands for 109th bead, which is known as the Sumeru bead. This is how the Ship of Gilgamesh matches perfectly with the Ship of Noah.

There is one conjunction of Jupiter with Saturn every 20 years (average 7253.46 days). This phenomenon is known as the great conjunction. There is one orbit of the North node of the moon (Rahu) around the Earth in 18.61 years (6798 days). The value of 16 orbits of Rahu matches the value of 15 great conjunctions. That is why 16 rounds of Japa Mala in a day are advised for Vaishnavas.

Three Arrows of Khatu Shyamji

There is a story linked with Mahabharata & it is related to Barbarika, son of Gatotkacha. Barbarika claimed to have completed the war of Mahabharata by using his 3 divine arrows. The 3 arrows of Barbarika are the 3 types of cycles of Sun, which cuts the orbital period of all the planets.

This prince Barbarika is known as Khatu Shyamji & his temple is located in Sikar district of Rajasthan.

Our Sun is always active like a human heart. Solar activity follows 3 types of periodic cycles-

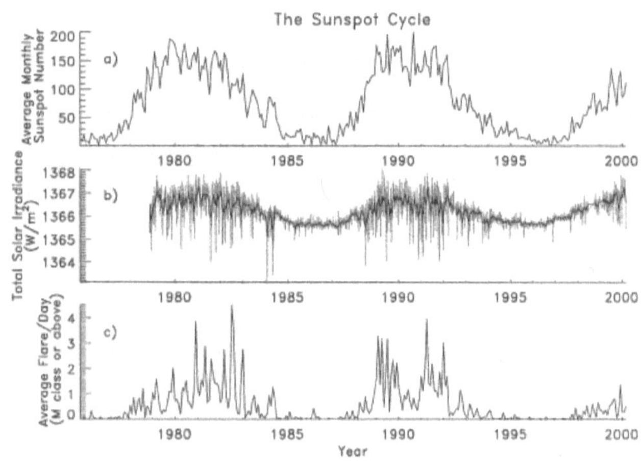

(Image courtesy: NASA)

1. Overall activity cycle of an average of 11 years (called Schwabe cycle).

    This cycle is remembered by Vaishnavas through fasting on every Ekadashi, the eleventh day from the new moon & full moon. In Puranas, there is a story that mentions Dhruva. Dhruva follows austerity & does penance in the name of Lord Vishnu. When He arrives at the age of 5 & a half years, Lord Vishnu appears before Him.

This period of 5 & 1/2 years is half of the 11-year period. Due to Lord Vishnu's blessing, Dhruva later becomes Dhruva Tara or Pole star.

Planet Mercury follows this cycle & does 137 orbits around the Sun in 3 cycles of 11 years. Important to note that 1/137 is fine- structure constant.

Our Earth follows this cycle & does 11 orbits around Sun (That is 11 years) in one cycle.

2. Sunspot cycle of average 95.115 days.

    There is a mention of the periodicity of 96 in Aarthi in praise of Lord Jagadish as *'bhakta jano ke sankat chiname door kare'* Where chiname means 96.

    There is also a mention of a period of 25 years cycle in the Rajasthani folk song 'Pacchiso Kal.'

    When we combine above 2, we find that in 25 years there are 96 periodicities of 95.115 days each. The number of daily Sunspots increase & decrease during an average period of 95.115 days.

    Planet Mercury follows this cycle & does 40 orbits around the Sun in 37 cycles of 95.115 days.

Our Earth follows this cycle & does 25 orbits around the Sun (That is 25 years) in 96 cycles.

Planet Mars follows this cycle & does 9 orbits around the Sun in 65 cycles.

Planet Jupiter follows this cycle & does 101 orbits around the Sun in 4600 cycles.

3. Solar flare cycle of average 112 days.

The solar flare cycle is a repetitive period of an average of 112 days when the intensity of the flares of the sun increases & decreases. This is remembered in Hindu Pachanga as Choghadiyas. In a day there are 8 choghadiyas of average one & a half hour each & there are 8 choghadiyas during a night.

If we calculate the number of choghadiyas for a week, we find that there are 56 choghadiyas during 7 days & 56 during 7 nights. This means a total of 112 choghadiyas in a week.

दिन की चौघड़ियां							रात की चौघड़ियां						
रवि	सोम	मंगल	बुध	गुरु	शुक्र	शनि	रवि	सोम	मंगल	बुध	गुरु	शुक्र	शनि
उद्वेग	अमृत	रोग	लाभ	शुभ	चर	काल	शुभ	चर	काल	उद्वेग	अमृत	रोग	लाभ
चर	काल	उद्वेग	अमृत	रोग	लाभ	शुभ	अमृत	रोग	लाभ	शुभ	चर	काल	उद्वेग
लाभ	शुभ	चर	काल	उद्वेग	अमृत	रोग	चर	काल	उद्वेग	अमृत	रोग	लाभ	शुभ
अमृत	रोग	लाभ	शुभ	चर	काल	उद्वेग	रोग	लाभ	शुभ	चर	काल	उद्वेग	अमृत
काल	उद्वेग	अमृत	रोग	लाभ	शुभ	चर	काल	उद्वेग	अमृत	रोग	लाभ	शुभ	चर
शुभ	चर	काल	उद्वेग	अमृत	रोग	लाभ	लाभ	शुभ	चर	काल	उद्वेग	अमृत	रोग
रोग	लाभ	शुभ	चर	काल	उद्वेग	अमृत	उद्वेग	अमृत	रोग	लाभ	शुभ	चर	काल
उद्वेग	अमृत	रोग	लाभ	शुभ	चर	काल	शुभ	चर	काल	उद्वेग	अमृत	रोग	लाभ

Planet Venus follows this cycle & does 01 orbit around the Sun in 2 cycle of 112 days.

Dwarf planet ceres follows this cycle & orbits one time around the Sun in 15 cycles of 112 days.

Planet Uranus follows this cycle & orbits one time around the Sun in 274 cycles. It is important to note that 274 is double the fine-structure constant.

The transit cycle of Mercury is formed when Mercury or the Sun is eclipsed when viewed from Earth. This is a period of 46 years & when it is divided by 150, the result is 112.

4. Joint cycle of Sunspots cycle of 95.115 days & Solar flare cycle of 112 days.

    When we multiply 95.115 by 112, we find a period of 10652.9 days or 29.1666 years.

    Various planets orbit around the sun in accordance with the above cycle of 29.1666 years, as below:

    Our Earth follows this cycle & does 175 orbits around the Sun (That is 175 years) in 6 cycles of 10652.9 days.

In western scriptures, Abraham's age is stated as 175 years.

In the epic Mahabharata, this period of 175 years (multiple 95.115 with 112) is set against the period of 275 years (multiple 95.115 X 96 with 11).

It is divided by 25 to form the ratio of 7:11, where 25-year sunspot cycle represents one akshuhini sena (army). Pandavas had 7 akshuhini army & they fought against Kauravas, who had 11 akshuhini army. The Pandavas won the battle in such a way that both armies were completely destroyed. It is important to note that the word Pandava is derived from The Kingdom of Pontus, Established around 281 BC in modern Turkey. The word Kauravas is derived from the King Cyrus (Kurus) of Persia, born around 600 BC in modern Iran. Kaurava means descendants of Kuru.

The ratio of 11:7 is half of the Pie, which is 22/7. When the Pie is multiplied by the diameter, we get the Perimeter of a Circle. Planets move around the Sun in a circular manner. Krishnadwepayana Vyasa, who wrote the epic Mahabharata, got his name Vyasa from this formula, Where Vyas in Sanskrit means diameter.

Planet Saturn follows this cycle & does 100 orbits around the Sun in 101 cycles.

Planet Neptune follows this cycle & does 177 orbits around the Sun in 1000 cycles.

There is mention of this cycle of 1000 in Kundalini yoga, as ultimate chakra or Sahasar chakra. Where Sahastra means one thousand. Since, Neptune is the outermost planet, this chakra is ultimate or topmost.

Also, the color of this chakra is same as the color of Neptune.

Dwarf planet Pluto follows this cycle & does 2 orbits around the Sun in 17 cycles.

Dwarf planet Eris follows this cycle & does 6 orbits around the Sun in 115 cycles.

Other than the orbit around the sun, the Schwabe cycle matches the movement of the moon around the Earth-

There are 34 lunar years in 3 × 11 solar years (that is in 33 solar years) on Earth. This is why there are 33 koti (type of) Gods mentioned in Puranas.

Thirty-three verities of Gods mentioned in Hindu scriptures are the deities of 33 solar years. Also, notable here is that there are a total of 68 Kshatriya castes of the lunar race & they consider themselves descendants of Lord Chandra (the moon). 68 is double of 34 lunar years.

The lunar North node (Rahu) orbits around the Earth in 6798.4 days & the same is true for the orbit of the lunar South Node (Ketu) around the Earth. The behaviour of both nodes is almost the same. They are the reason behind eclipses. So, we can divide this period of 6798.4 days by 2 to arrive at a period of 3399.2 days. This value of 3399.2 days is compared with the 11-year Schwabe cycle, which is 4017.66 days. When we divide both values by 103, then we get a ratio of 33:39. Also, it is important to note here that there are 103 subcastes under Pareek Brahmins & Pareek's claims themselves descendants of Vyasa. The square root of the Sunspot cycle of 95.115 days & solar flare cycle of 112 days is 103 days, with a difference of 1.5 Lunation in total.

A curious mind will always wonder if there is a common point in time when all 3 solar cycles meet.

When we multiply the 275-year period (which is a multiple of 11 years & 95.115 days cycles) by 20, we get a period of 2008832 days. This period is also divisible by 112 days. 2008832 days is a period of 5500 years. This is the meeting point of the 3 Solar cycles.

There is a western religious book, which is named 'The First Book of Adam & Eve.' In this book, God says to Adam that he will give Adam the Fruit of the Tree of Life after 5500 years.

This means that all the 3 cycles were identified by the writers of the Scriptures thousands of years ago.

But that is not all. The period of 5500 years is not divisible by the joint cycle of Sunspots cycle of 95.115 days & Solar flare cycle of 112 days.

To achieve this divisility, we have to multiply 5500 years with 14. Now we have a figure of

77000 years. This period is divisible by both 175 years & 275 years.

The 14 periodicities of 5500 years each are called 14- Bhuvana (Bhuvana means rotation of a disk- specifically a wooden disk mounted over a well & used to pull water from the well). In various books, 14 bhuvanas are mentioned as 14 different places, which is not correct. Infect they are 14 periods of time.

Then, Tribhvana or 3 lokas are mentioned.

The Chalukya King Vikramaditya VI, who ruled around 1100 CE, adopted the title of Tribhuvan Malla or Lord of 3 lokas.

A period of full circle of Earth's Precession of Equinox is about 25700 years, wherein the Earth's 23.5-degree tilt changes its direction over the period of time. A period of 77000 years is around 3 times the 25700 years. This is why the same period of 77000 years is known as 14 bhuvana as well as Tribhuvana or Triloki.

When 77000 is divided by 11, 25, and 112, we get a result of 2.5; & This is why one of the earliest Islamic monuments in India, 'Adhai din ka Jopara,' which is located in Ajmer, is named after this result. Where adhai means 2 & half. Similarly, fifteenth-century poet Kabir sang-

Dhai Akshar prem ka padhe so pandith hoye

Meaning that one who understands 2 & half syllables of love becomes the learned one.

There is a system of religious donation in Islam known as Zakah, wherein people donate 2.5% of their Income. This figure of 2.5% is derived from the above result of 2.5.

As per Hindu scripture, there are 4 Yugas in the happening of the time. Four yuga combined is called a Mahayuga. The period of 77000 years itself is a Mahayuga. The 4 yuga periods are as follows-

Satya yuga; 30800 years

Treta yuga; 23100 years

Dvapara yuga; 15400 years

Kali yuga; 7700 years

When 30800 is divided by 11, 25, and 112, we get a result of 1. This is why it is said that Satya yuga has 4 legs.

When 23100 is divided by 11, 25, and 112, we get a result of 3/4. This is why it is said that Treta yuga has 3 legs.

When 15400 is divided by 11, 25, 112 we get a result as 1/2. This is why it is said that Dvapara yuga has 2 legs.

When 7700 is divided by 11, 25, and 112, we get a result of 1/4. This is why Kali yuga is said to have one leg.

The total number of 4 yugas is 77000 years. The basic unit of the yuga cycle is 7700 years. There are 10 cycles of 7700 years in total & 10 incarnations of Lord Vishnu are the deities of each cycle of 7700 years.

But this is still incomplete, as the period of 77000 years is not divisible by a period of 32 years of Yoginis or 33 years of 33 koti devatas. To achieve this divisibility, we have to multiply this by 2.4.

Now, we have a period of 184800 years, which fulfils the criteria. When divided it by a period of 7700, we get 24 as a result. This is why there are a total of 24 incarnations of Lord Vishnu. Similarly, there are 24 Tirthankaras in Jainism. Also, there is mention of 24 Gurus of Dattatreya. When we divide 184800 with 33 & then 100, the result is 56 years. This is why Lord Krishna is offered 56 types of foods, called Chhappan Bhog.

We have discussed so much about numbers. Now the question arises: is there any relation between these numbers & actual happenings on Earth? To verify this, we will compare these with Milankovitch cycles.

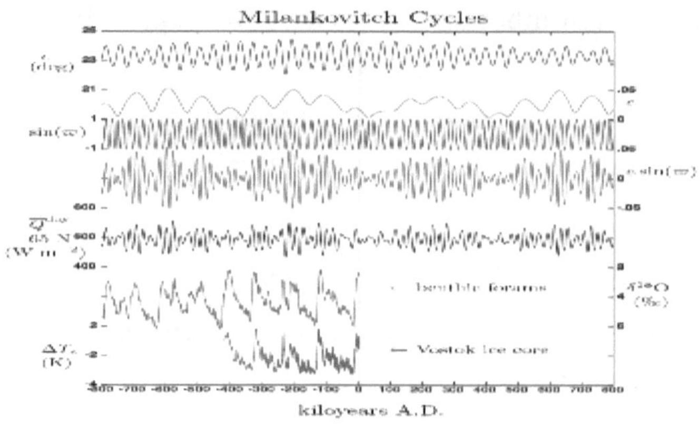

(Image courtesy Wikipedia)

First Milankovitch cycle is about periodic variations in Axial tilt of the Earth. Axial tilt of Earth with respect to its orbital path around sun does very over a period of time in cyclic manner, where average value of a cycle is 41025.6 years. The period of 184800 years, when multiplied with 0.999 & 02 & then divided by 09, we get 41025.6.

Earth's eccentricity is the oval shape of its orbit around the Sun when compared to a perfect circle. Over the period of time, the shape of the orbit varies & this happens in a cyclic manner with a cycle period of an average of 94117.65 years. The value of 09 cycles of 94117.65 years is equal to 11 X 77000.

The longitude of the perihelion of Earth also changes with a periodic cycle of 21621.621 years. When the period of 184800 years is divided by 0.033 & then 259, we get 21621.621 as a result.

Earth's Precession index is a measurement of Earth's closeness to the Sun when it is summer season on Earth's equator. The Precession index follows 2 patterns. One short-term cycle of 21621.621 years, which is the same as that of the Longitude of perihelion. Second, a long-term cycle of an average of 106666.67 years. In 400 periods of 184800, there are 693 periods of 106666.67 years.

Three times the period of 106666.67 years is also divisible by the average synodic period cycle of internal planets of 32 years by 10000.

Daily average insolation (sunlight) on the summer solstice on Earth follows the same double cycles as the Earth's Precession index.

Russian agency has built a station at Vostok Ice Lake in Antarctica to study Earth's atmosphere. They have drilled the Ice in the Ice Lake, taken samples & studied the same for dissolved carbon dioxide & Methane content in the Ice from zero to 3300 meters. This Ice has been deposited in the lake for the last 420000 years. It is important to note here that both carbon dioxide & Methane are greenhouse gases, which have an impact on Earth's atmospheric temperature.

The peak dissolved carbon dioxide level in the Ice during the above period follows 2 types of cycles. A long-term cycle of an average of 105000 years & a short-term peak cycle of an average of 5833.33 years. Both the periods of these cycles are divisible by the joint period of Sunspots & solar flares, which is 29.1666 years. The 105000 years cycle is divisible by 3600 times & the 5833.33 years cycle is divisible by 200 times. The same pattern is followed by dissolved Methane. The above 105000 years period is in 15:11 ratio with 77000 years period.

Now we can understand that the yuga periods have a clear impact on Earth's various cyclic periodicities & climatic changes. And this is how God acts as Kaal or Time.

God As Universal Consciousness

Our body is controlled by our brain. The brain is the central part of our nervous system. The nervous system works by transferring information mainly through sodium ions. Our moon & planet Mercury have sodium ion tails. So, the moon is called as presiding deity of Emotions, Mood & Mind. At the same time, Mercury or Buddha is called the Lord of Buddhi or Intellect.

All the planets including Sun have got one or more kind of tail- either magnetic, ion or gas tail. This means that there is some kind of mechanism available with planets for transferring information.

Our Earth has got a sodium layer in its atmosphere. This is situated at an altitude between 90 km & 100 km. Its thickness is about 5 km. The sodium layer of the Earth is larger than the total size of all the oceans. The sodium layer is yellow coloured. This is why Lord Krishna, who represent the Earth is called as Pitamberdhari, meaning one who wears yellow clothings.

There are observations that can prove the existence of something that manages the whole system around us in the same manner as our brain manages our body.

All of us get dreams while sleeping. Most of the dreams are not relevant & hence forgotten immediately; some are forgotten later. But very few dreams are actually related to our lives or to the lives of our known people. These Dreams are really important to us.

For example, I will quote some of the Dreams which later proved to be true-

In 2009, I was living in Bangalore; one night, while asleep, I had a dream that I was being fined by traffic police for my two-wheeler in the area of Gandhi Nagar in Bangalore. I used to go to Gandhinagar only once a month to file monthly value-added tax returns. This time, I avoided the trip to Gandhi Nagar & instead sent my office staff to file the Return. Later, I got some notice from value-added tax authorities about differences in tax assessments. This time, I could not avoid it because it was an important matter. I went to the value-added tax office. Gandhi Nagar was a crowded area. Somehow, I got space & parked my Two-wheeler & filed my answer to the tax authorities.

By the time I came back, traffic police had towed my two-wheeler for parking it in a No-parking zone. Finally, I had to pay some amount as a fine.

Advance information about future events had come to my subconscious mind when I was sleeping. This happened when the subconscious mind was active & conscious mind was inactive.

My use of the term subconscious mind is for the part of the mind which manages the working of essential bodily activities like metabolism, heartbeat, respiration, etc, which are not under our control. The subconscious mind is always active. Whereas the conscious mind stands for the part of the mind which manages our thinking & actions about which we are aware & which is under our control. The conscious mind is more active when we are awake & has little activeness when we are asleep.

This kind of advance information dreamt could either be stored in our physical body or it may available in nature surrounding us. But approximate geo-positioning of the dreamed action favours its availability in nature surrounding us. But since it is about self, its origin from physical body cannot be written off.

There is another example-

In the year 1994, while sleeping, I had a dream that my maternal grandfather had expired. I live in Karnataka, which is 2000 km away from the place in Rajasthan where my maternal grandfather lived. There was no phone call or other communication prior to the dream. He was enjoying good health.

The next day evening, there was a phone call from one of our relatives, & by chance, I lifted the phone. The relative informed Me that my maternal grandfather had died in the morning.

This dream shows that the information is transferred from the nature surrounding us to the subconscious mind. But since the subject person is genetically related & genetic code is available inside our body, its origin from the our physical body cannot be written off.

The last example-

Many years back, my grandfather's younger brother got a dream that a person from our nearby town had won the election of Sarpanch (Village Head) & come to our village riding on a Horse.

Grandfather went to that person & informed him about the dream. He did not take it seriously & said that He does not even has a Horse.

A few days later, there were elections. The above person filed his nomination. It is important to note that he was allotted Horse as electoral symbol & He won the election.

This dream confirms that the information is transferred from the nature surrounding us to the subconscious mind. Since the subject person is not related & his genetic code is not available inside the body of the dreaming person, its origin from the physical body is completely written off.

This clearly indicates that there is a transfer of information from the nature surrounding us to our subconscious mind. Though the mechanism of transfer of information from the nature surrounding us to our subconscious mind is not available, the existence of such advanced information itself is more important than the mechanism of transfer of information. This indicates the existence of nature surrounding us is a single living entity.

Let's try to create a model of the nature surrounding us & Ourself as a part of whole existence, both being a living entity.

The mind of the nature surrounding us is like a multidimensional ocean. The subconscious mind of a living being is like a ripple or a wave of that ocean. The ocean as a whole is immortal, but the wave has a lifespan. For a human being, the life span is around a hundred years. Our predecessor/ ancestor is the wave preceding our own wave & our successors/offspring are the waves following ours. A wave is connected with the ocean, so the information is transferred from the ocean to the wave. Our mind cannot correctly translate every piece of information from the nature surrounding us, so all dreams are not translated into reality. If a yogi who has perfected his life or a person who has a good connection with the universal mind tries to get some past or future information about anybody, he may do so.

Our mind is the most volatile thing, and so is the mind of Mother nature. The water of the ocean becomes volatile & shows effects like high tides & low tides due to the gravitational force of the moon & Sun. That is why the cycles of the moon & sun have an impact on the life cycles, like birth, mating, etc, of the animals living in the Sea. Similarly, the activities of the Sun & movement of various planets create an impact on the mind of nature (the Earth) due to various forces like magnetic force and gravitational forces. In the same way, the position of the planets impacts the subconscious mind of a living being, based on the position of the planets at the time of the creation of his DNA, that is, the time of mating of his/ her parents or the time of pairing or 2 parental RNAs.

This is why omniscient rishi Parashara, seeing the position of planets & nakshatras, mated with Satyavati to father a great rishi like Veda Vyasa.

The position of planets & nakshatras at the time of pairing of 2 RNAs decides all the course of life including time of birth of the individual. It's like the force imposed on the water at the time of origin of a ripple in water decides the intensity & lifespan of the Ripple.

Remember, the above statements are about the subconscious mind of a living being.

What we do with a conscious mind depends on what we learn from our parents, teachers & people surrounding us & how we implement these learnings by making various decisions & doing various deeds.

Then, a question arises- What is Atma?

The word Atma has got common root with the word atom. The Greek word Atmos is common link between the two. Atom is the basic unit of any element. In general, it cannot be destroyed, it does not decay & its immortal. So is quoted for Atma.

In fact, our DNA is our Atma. DNA differentiates any living being from the rest of the world. Yudhishthira answered Yaksha that a son is holding the Atma of his father. That is why son or Daughter is called Atmaj or Atmaja. It is said in the scriptures-

'*Atmaiva putro jayate*'

The offspring hold the RNA of each Parent in the chromosomes of their DNA. It is only through his/ her offspring that the Atma of a person is alive in a subtle form & it is immortal. If a person does intentionally or unintentionally adapt Brahmacharya, does not marry & does not produce offspring, then He is liberated from the cycle of birth & death, or he attains Moksha.

A question arises: what does pass away when a person dies? The answer to that is when Prana pass away from the body of a person, then the person dies. Prana is the action of breathing by the lungs.

Then question arises, who is the God. Before we consider someone as the God. We should understand that He must be connected with & have impact over all the beings.

As far as I think, the Earth is the primary God. Then- the Sun, the Moon, the Planets, and the Sky are Gods.

It means everything around us is part of God. Movements of planets, asterism & their position from a given place at a given point in time are the cause of the creation of ripples in this Ocean & are the cause behind happenings in the subconscious minds of all beings. Only the conscious mind is the source of free will. The surroundings react to us based upon our actions, & our actions are based on both the subconscious mind & conscious mind. This is how a Being is connected with the God.